Life-Saving Strategies
for New Teachers

School Renaissance Institute, Inc.
Madison, Wisconsin

D1069682

School Renaissance Institute
P.O. Box 45016
Madison, WI 53744-5016
(800) 200-4848

Printed in the United States of America

ISBN 1-893751-88-0

Writing and editing by Dottie Raymer
Illustrations by George Sebok

Cover art: Special thanks to the following artists for their drawings. Right top corner: Francine Lease; Top row left to right: Monica Fallen; Shawn Kroll. Bottom row left to right: Bih Zama; Tireah Rinzel; Breanna Wilson.

8/00

Contents

Staying Afloat

Handling Students

Introduction

You did it! The hours of required coursework and classroom observations, and the rigors of student teaching, have finally paid off. You have a teaching job!

Now what?

As a new teacher, you bring rare qualities to your classroom—a fresh outlook, new energy, and a clear faith that your best intentions will rule the day. At the same time, you've heard the rumors of others' first years of teaching:

"It's a trial by fire. No one told me what to do."

"I was thrown to the wolves."

"I was completely isolated. Student teaching never prepared me for this."

The statistics are disheartening. Nationwide, 30 percent of new teachers leave the profession within the first two years. More than half leave within seven years.

What makes one new teacher sink, and another not only swim but enjoy the swimming? Successful new teachers consistently report that what makes or breaks the first year of teaching often comes down to a few simple strategies they discovered to manage the overwhelming day-to-day challenges of teaching. When new teachers moan at the end of the year, "Why didn't someone tell me?" it is usually one of those life-saving strategies they are moaning about.

The routines and strategies in this book are not new. Most are "tricks of the trade" that seasoned teachers have been using for years. These strategies won't make you love teaching—only your own optimism, creativity, and love of children will do that. They will, however, give you the confidence and control you need to do the job you are hired to do—teach your students well.

The Golden Rules

One of the most valuable lessons that experience teaches is how to distinguish what is important from what is not. As a new teacher, you will likely feel overwhelmed and frustrated by others' expectations of and demands on you. The office wants those forms filled out now. A parent expects you to return his phone call as soon as possible. A student's behavior demands action immediately. You know that how and when you react to each of these situations is important. But how can you possibly do it all?

The six strategies that follow form the foundation of successful teaching. Together, they will provide a guideline for you to use whenever you are feeling frustrated or overwhelmed. Read these strategies first, and return to them often. Like the wisdom that comes from experience, these guiding principles will help you decide what to do and when to do it.

1 Find a mentor.

Seasoned teachers will tell you that teaching is the only profession in which a beginner is expected to do the same work as a veteran—and with equal success!

New teachers, alone in their classrooms, often complain of feeling isolated and "at sea" in their new environment. At times like these, the wisdom, guidance, and sympathy of an experienced colleague can be invaluable.

Some schools pair new teachers with veterans in a formal mentoring system. In others, new teachers must find mentors on their own. Whether the mentoring system in your school is formal or informal, try to find—before school starts, if possible—someone who can give you answers to your nuts-and-bolts questions about the school and the curriculum ("How do I work the copy machine?" "Which textbooks should I use?"). Take some time to find someone you can trust to answer your more difficult or sensitive questions ("Will the principal back my discipline procedure?").

Where do you find this wellspring of wisdom? Here are some suggestions:

- ✔ Get to know other teachers at your grade level or in your content area.
- ✔ Ask for recommendations from teachers who have recently been through the mentoring process.
- ✔ Set aside one planning period each month to observe a veteran teacher in action.
- ✔ Volunteer for team teaching situations with veteran teachers.
- ✔ Attend professional meetings and conferences, and arrange to carpool with other teachers from your school.

2 | Set specific goals.

Before school begins, take some time to think about precisely what you want your students to accomplish by the end of the year. Use your district curriculum materials, state standards, and current textbooks to help guide your thinking. State your goals as specifically as possible:

> **Vague (and probably unachievable) goal:** I hope to cover the material in the Grade 3 math text.
> **Specific (and probably achievable) goal:** Students will memorize multiplication facts through the 9s table.

Write your list of goals and an approximate timeline in the back of your planning book or journal, and make copies of the list to share with students and parents. As the year progresses, these goals provide a structure for your teaching. The more aligned your teaching is with your end goals, and the more your students know what you expect them to learn, the greater all your chances are for achieving success.

3 | Overplan.

Carpenters have a maxim about the need for careful planning: "Measure twice; cut once." A variation of that saying for teachers could be "Prepare twice; teach once." The key to surviving your first few months of teaching lies in overpreparation.

- ✔ As a rule of thumb, plan two hours' worth of material for every hour of actual class time.
- ✔ Plan at least one alternate approach for each major lesson objective.
- ✔ Try to collect all materials and make all copies the week before you will use them. Never assume that you can make copies on the morning you are to give the lesson.
- ✔ Keep a folder or card file of "filler" activities—games, puzzles, and other brain-stretchers to have at your fingertips for unexpected extra moments.

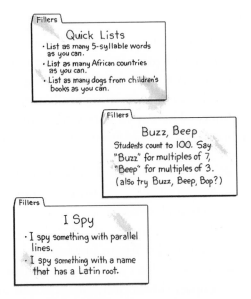

Fillers

Quick Lists
- List as many 5-syllable words as you can.
- List as many African countries as you can.
- List as many dogs from children's books as you can.

Fillers

Buzz, Beep
Students count to 100. Say "Buzz" for multiples of 7, "Beep" for multiples of 3. (also try Buzz, Beep, Bop?)

Fillers

I Spy
- I spy something with parallel lines.
- I spy something with a name that has a Latin root.

Keep a file of "filler" activities to keep students actively involved during spare moments.

4 Rely on routines.

Students (and teachers) function best in a predictable environment. Too often, however, school life is anything but predictable. Do what you can to make your classroom an oasis of order. Post each day's schedule and assignments in the same place every day and establish routines for completing regular tasks such as:

✔ Beginning and ending the school day or class period (see strategies 16 and 17)
✔ Gaining students' attention (see strategy 18)
✔ Giving help to individual students (see strategy 33)
✔ Collecting or passing out papers (see strategy 24)

Plan to use class time to teach students important procedures during the first days of school (see strategy 19).

Morning Routine

1. Hang up jacket.
2. Put attendance card in correct lunchbox.
3. Empty backpack. Make sure you have:
   Language arts folder
   Math book
   Independent reading book
   Assignment notebook
   Binder
   2 pencils
4. Put homework and forms in correct boxes.
5. Begin opening activity.

Post the steps of common procedures for easy reference.

5 Expect respect.

One of the most painful lessons new teachers learn is that they can't be their students' friend.

Positive teacher-student relationships are built on trust and respect, not friendship. Recognize the imbalance of power that naturally exists between you and your students. Whether you feel comfortable with the role or not, you are the authority. Your students need you to be an authority they can admire and respect.

- ✔ Dress as a professional. Clean, pressed clothes signal to your students that you mean business. Invest in a well-tailored black or navy blue blazer. You won't be sorry.
- ✔ Expect students to use a title of respect (Mr., Ms., Mrs., or Dr.) when they address you.
- ✔ Maintain a businesslike atmosphere in

the classroom. Don't use class time to snack, knit, balance your checkbook, or check your e-mail.

✔ Require students to follow classroom procedures (see strategy 4) and your discipline policy (see strategy 9) from the very beginning.

✔ Treat students with the same respect you expect. Always say "please" and "thank you."

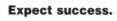

6 Expect success.

When asked why they chose the teaching profession, most teachers will give a similar answer—to affect the lives of children. More than anything else you do during your teaching career, your own expectations will affect your students' learning.

- ✔ Be specific about your expectations. If you don't give your students specific criteria for success, their chances for success will be hit or miss.
- ✔ Catch your students in the act of succeeding, and comment on their success: "Thank you, Mark, for coming into the room so quietly."
- ✔ Praise publicly. Criticize privately.
- ✔ Remember that words can hurt. Never use sarcasm or humiliation when correcting a student.
- ✔ Teach your students, not your subject. If your students aren't succeeding, change what you are doing.

But What Do I Do on Monday?

No matter how strong your teacher-training program was or how much time you've had to prepare, the first day of school for any new teacher is always a shock. Nothing can prepare you for the four extra students for whom you have no desks, or the special-needs student whose classroom aide quit yesterday, or the mountains of forms that must be returned to the school office by 9 A.M.

The strategies and routines that follow will help answer some of your most pressing questions: "What do I do first?" "How can I maintain control in the classroom?" "How do I build rapport with my students?" "What do I say to parents?" Read through these strategies, and then choose and adapt those that best fit your own needs. Every one of these strategies will make your daily life in the classroom run more smoothly.

7

Sketch an outline of the year's curriculum.

"Just stay a page ahead of the students!" So goes one platitude about teaching. As any seasoned teacher will tell you, however, trying to stay just a page ahead of the students is one of the most stressful teaching methods imaginable!

Navigating the perilous seas of teaching is difficult enough without having to guess where you are going. Do all you can to become familiar with the required curriculum *before school begins*.

- ✔ Ask for a copy of your state standards or district's grade-level curriculum. (Most states and districts have standards posted on the Internet.)
- ✔ Peruse the textbooks and other teaching materials you will be using.
- ✔ Review your own goals for the year (see strategy 2).

Next, identify your major units of study in each curriculum area. Don't expect to "cover" the entire textbook or curriculum plan. Assume that you will have to make some choices about what you can teach well in the time you have allotted. Buy or make a school-year calendar, and block off sections of time for each major unit. Use the calendar to help you keep on track as the school year progresses.

8 Set up a record-keeping system.

Set up your grading system or student record book before the first day of school.

If your school has a district-mandated record-keeping system, take some time to learn how to use it before school starts. If the system is computerized, ask for a tutoring session and, if possible, arrange to install the software on your home computer.

Before you choose or develop your own record-keeping system, list the different types of information you will need to record. Elementary teachers who record anecdotal information may want to use a loose-leaf notebook or Rolodex® file divided into sections for each child. Secondary teachers may prefer a spreadsheet with separate columns for daily and cumulative scores.

Ms. Sanchez Grade 4 Math ✓ = Completed ○ = Absent			Page 42 1-10	Page 45 All	Quiz - Multiplication
#	Student's Name	Phone	Cumulative Grade	10/15	10/16	10/18
1	Alvarez, Alicia	592-1420	95	✓	✓	95
2	Brown, Tim	838-6622	60	○	✓	60
3	Demming, Sam	592-1673		✓	✓	○
4	Garcia, Rico	284-4949	85	✓	✓	85
5	Kelly, Patricia	838-7254	90	✓	✓	90

Think about the types of information you want to record. Then choose the record-keeping method that best fits your needs.

9 | **Develop a discipline plan.**

The most important lesson you can teach your students during the first weeks of school is how to behave appropriately. View the time you spend developing and teaching key disciplinary rules as an investment in your students' learning and the smooth functioning of your classroom.

Make sure you have a clear understanding of your school's discipline policy. Then write down the behaviors you feel are imperative for maintaining a positive, productive learning environment in your own classroom. Choose no more than five important rules and state them as specific behaviors. For example:

- ✔ Listen quietly to directions.
- ✔ Keep your hands, feet, and objects to yourself.
- ✔ Be in your seat when the bell rings.

✔ No swearing or put-downs.
✔ Ask permission before leaving the room.

Next, develop a list of consequences for breaking the rules. Some teachers place checks next to the violator's name on the chalkboard. Others use a hole-punch to make holes in an index card with the child's name on it. Whatever system you use, make sure that your students understand the consequences of their actions. For example:

✔ First violation (one check or hole): verbal warning
✔ Second violation (two checks or holes): 5 minutes' detention during lunch
✔ Third violation (three checks or holes): 15 minutes' detention after school and a phone call home

In many classrooms, students also earn rewards by accumulating tally marks, chips, or classroom scrip (one teacher calls his "Heebie Jeebies") for good behavior.

Make sure that you have administrative support for your discipline plan. Then post the plan in a prominent place in the classroom and send a copy home for both students and their parents to sign.

Dear Parents:

Class 6C has a simple discipline plan that all students are expected to follow for the comfort and safety of all. Please read and discuss this plan with your child and sign below to indicate your support. Thank you.

Classroom Rules

1. Listen quietly to directions.
2. Keep your hands, feet, and objects to yourself.
3. Be in your seat when the bell rings.
4. No swearing or put-downs.
5. Ask permission before leaving the room.

Consequences for Choosing to Break a Rule

1. First violation: verbal warning
2. Second violation: 10 minutes' detention
3. Third violation: 30 minutes' detention after school and phone call home
4. Fourth violation: 60 minutes' detention and referral to the principal
5. Severe disruption: Immediate referral to the principal

We understand this discipline plan and will support it.

Student Signature: *Ellen McNeil*

Parent Signature: *[signature]*

Make sure that your students and their parents understand and sign your discipline plan.

10 Start a filing system.

Attendance, lunch counts, lesson plans, assignments, student records, government forms. How can you keep track of them all without adding another eight hours to your workday? Before school begins, set up a filing system to help you cope with the paper chase.

- ✔ Make a file for each student. Anything pertaining to that student—notes about behavior, samples of work, parental communications—will go into that file.
- ✔ Keep a separate file for each month. File time-sensitive notices and lesson ideas under the proper month. At the beginning of each month, check the file to help you plan.
- ✔ For each unit you teach, keep a three-ring binder in which you file all the lesson plans, handouts, and assignments you use.

11

Arrange your room to reduce distractions.

The way you arrange the furniture in your classroom directly affects student behavior. Plan the arrangement carefully to avoid distractions and focus your students' attention.

- ✔ Before school starts, count the number of desks you need. Request two extra desks for students who register late.
- ✔ Start the year with assigned seating. Assigning seats allows you to confirm that you have enough desks and is a good way to get a head start on memorizing students' names.
- ✔ Begin with desks in rows or a semicircle facing the blackboard or other teaching area. This arrangement is the least distracting and allows ample aisle room for you to move around and work with individuals.

- ✔ Sit in desks placed in different positions to make sure that each student has a clear view of the teaching area.
- ✔ Place desks as far away as possible from distracting areas such as the door, pencil sharpener, and computer.
- ✔ Place your desk at the back of the room where you have a good view of students but they are less likely to be distracted by your work with others.

Finally, plan where students will keep their belongings. If individual lockers or cubbies are not available, ask a local ice cream store to save large ice cream cartons for you. Shoe boxes and cereal boxes with the tops cut off also work well.

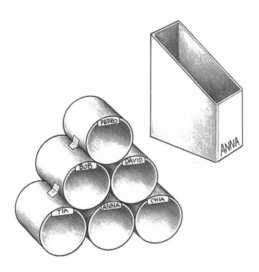

You can make cubbies for students' belongings out of large ice cream cartons or cereal boxes.

12 Arrange supplies so that they are accessible.

Use the list of suggested supplies on pages 96–97 to help you gather a set of basic materials for your classroom. Find out where supplies are stored in your school and learn the procedure for obtaining what you need. If you don't see what you need, don't be afraid to ask for it. Remember, you are a professional and have a right to request the appropriate tools of your trade.

Even teachers with large classroom budgets find that there are some supplies that can be obtained only through the fine art of scavenging. Keep your eyes open for good sources of free and inexpensive supplies, such as yard sales and thrift stores. Use containers such as shoe boxes, dishpans, and margarine containers to organize your materials. Label the containers and place supplies where they will be easily accessible.

Dear Parents and Guardians,

We are setting up an art center in our classroom so that we have materials available for our many projects throughout the year. Would you please look through the list below and send in whatever you have available? Thanks for your help!

Sincerely,
Mr. Garcia

- fabric scraps
- yarn
- egg cartons
- film canisters
- margarine containers
- juice or coffee cans
- old greeting cards
- wallpaper or gift wrap scraps
- toilet paper or paper towel rolls

Parents can be a good resource for classroom materials.

13   Make your walls work for you.

Walk into any teacher supply store with its rows of books filled with bulletin board ideas, and you might wonder, "Is this what makes a good teacher? Bulletin boards?" Then think back on the teachers who affected you most. Why were they wonderful? Was it because of their bulletin boards? Probably not.

Don't discount bulletin boards completely, however. As a teacher, you need every moment of the day, every inch of space, and every opportunity you can grab to teach. Even your walls can help, if you use them well.

✔ Use color backings or borders to separate boards and walls into distinct areas. If you have backing paper available, cover each board with two layers. In the middle of the year, when the first layer is torn and faded and the supply room is empty, you will be glad you did.

✔ Choose a permanent place for the daily schedule. Use different colored chalk or strips of poster board with Velcro® backing to designate different time blocks or activities.

✔ Designate one section of the blackboard for daily assignments.

✔ Post your discipline plan (see strategy 9) in a prominent place. Leave extra wall space for other classroom procedures you may want to post later (see strategy 4).

✔ Designate one section as the "Message Center" for school notices or daily reminders from you.

✔ Plan at least one first-week activity that will provide student work for display— for example, a "Me" collage or a large bookworm listing the books that students read over the summer (see page 95).

✔ Use one section to excite students' curiosity about one of the first topics they will be studying. For example, post photographs of strange sea animals with the caption "What Is This?" or brainteasers from the year's curriculum: "Do you know the answers to these questions? You will by June!"

Have students list their summer reading on caterpillar sections. Then use the sections to create a lively bulletin board during the first days of school.

14

Write a note or postcard to each student before school begins.

"Who'd ya get?" "What's she like?" For most students, getting to know a new teacher is one of the most frightening aspects of beginning a new school year. You can help smooth the transition (for your students *and* yourself!) by sending each student a brief note of welcome before school begins. Include in your note:

✔ a warm welcome
✔ a fun bit of information about yourself
✔ the date and times of the first day of school
✔ the room number and, if necessary, how to get there
✔ a list of school supplies that each student should bring on the first day

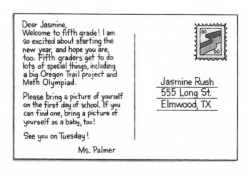

Dear Jasmine,
Welcome to fifth grade! I am so excited about starting the new year, and hope you are, too. Fifth graders get to do lots of special things, including a big Oregon Trail project and Math Olympiad.

Please bring a picture of yourself on the first day of school. If you can find one, bring a picture of yourself as a baby, too!

See you on Tuesday!

Ms. Palmer

Jasmine Rush
555 Long St.
Elmwood, TX

Get the school year off to a positive start by writing a short, friendly note to your students.

15

Try to speak with each student's parents within the first few weeks—before school starts, if possible.

For most new teachers, working with parents ranks right up there with maintaining discipline as a source of high anxiety. Yet everyone agrees that students perform better when their parents and teachers work together. Building the support and confidence of parents takes time, but it is well worth the effort.

A positive, informal conference at the beginning of the school year is a good place to start. Use the time to introduce yourself, to share schedules, and to encourage parents to keep in touch.

If possible, arrange to visit your students' homes. At the very least, make an effort to reach each parent by telephone. A short, friendly chat at the beginning of the year can make later, more difficult calls easier to handle.

16 **Welcome students at the door.**

You are in a new school, you are late for class, and you can't find the room where you are supposed to be. Anyone who has ever been in school has probably experienced some form of this classic anxiety dream; yet year after year, thousands of students replay exactly the same scenario.

You can do a lot to get the first day of school off to a good start simply by helping your students figure out whether they are in the right place.

✔ Post your name, room number, and grade level or subject on the classroom door and inside the classroom.
✔ Have the class roster handy so you can welcome students by name at the door. Preview the class roster and get help with pronunciation if necessary.
✔ Have a name tag (for younger students) or nameplate ready for each

student on the roster. Have extra materials available for students who may
have registered late.

✔ Help students find their assigned seats,
either by looking for their nameplates
or by checking a seating chart that you
have displayed.

✔ Smile!

Use simple cutouts or folded poster paper to make name tags or nameplates.

17 Give students an assignment to do right away on the first day.

The first minutes of the first day of school can be chaotic. Students wander in early or late. Parents linger with questions and concerns. Administrators interrupt with last-minute instructions.

Cut down on the chaos by having an activity ready for students to complete as soon as they enter the classroom. Post the assignment in the designated area on the board (see strategy 23) and lay out any necessary materials on each desk. Be sure that the activity you choose can be completed independently and successfully by every student. For example:

✔ Grades K–1: Students draw "Getting to Know You" pictures of themselves doing a favorite activity.

✔ Grades 2–3: Students create name tags for desks, lockers, or cubbies.

✔ Grades 4 and up: Students complete personal interest inventories.

18 Establish a routine for getting students' attention.

Of all the routines you will teach your students this year, the procedure for getting their attention is the most important. Teach this routine first, so you can begin reinforcing it immediately.

Choose the cue that you will use to gain students' attention carefully, because you will want to use the same cue from the first day forward. Some cues that teachers have found to be effective include:

- ✔ a bell or whistle
- ✔ a clapping sequence, which students repeat
- ✔ a phrase, such as "freeze, look, and listen"
- ✔ a slow count to 3 or 5
- ✔ a hand signal
- ✔ a short song or rhyme

19 Teach classroom routines during the first week.

Few teachers go into the profession for the joy of teaching classroom procedures. Research tells us, however, that the most successful teachers are those who spend a substantial amount of time doing just that: teaching the routines and rules that enable the class to run smoothly.

Use your class time during the first few days to teach at least these critical procedures:

✔ gaining students' attention
✔ discipline plan
✔ beginning and ending day

Plan lessons for classroom procedures as you would any other lesson, with objectives (e.g., "Identify the steps for beginning the school day."), instruction, and guided practice. Post the steps of each procedure and reinforce them whenever you have the opportunity.

20   Teach organizational skills.

When adults are disorganized, we talk about being overwhelmed. When students are disorganized, we scold them. Give your students the help they need to be organized. Teach basic organizational skills as you would any classroom routine (see strategy 19). It will make your students' lives—and yours—much easier.

- ✔ Plan how you want students to organize their work before school starts so that you can list any materials they need on their supplies list
- ✔ Have younger students keep papers that go home or must be returned in sturdy "take-home folders."
- ✔ From second grade on, require students to copy your posted assignments into an assignment notebook.
- ✔ Decide whether you want students to

use a spiral notebook or a section of loose-leaf binder for each subject. In elementary and middle school, require all your students to use the same system.

✔ Use calendars and checklists to teach students how to organize their time.

PROJECT PLANNER FOR __Nick__

TOPIC __Otters__

TASK:	MATERIALS:	COMPLETE BY:	DONE
Take notes	Encyclopedia Books, Internet	Mar. 5	✓
Outline	Outline form	Mar. 12	✓
First draft	pencil	Mar. 21	✓
Animal model	clay, cardboard	Mar. 30	
Final draft	blue or black pen	Mar. 30	

Teach students to manage their time by
dividing large projects into smaller tasks.

21 Learn your students' names as quickly as possible.

Nothing tells a student that you care about him more than calling him by his name.

- ✔ Use the student's name every time you speak to him.
- ✔ Require students to wear name tags for the first week to make it easier for students and staff alike to get acquainted.
- ✔ Make and use a seating chart.
- ✔ Take a picture of each student on the first day of school. Use the photos on your seating chart or on a "Getting to Know You" bulletin board.
- ✔ Play getting-acquainted games, such as a scavenger hunt in which students hunt for a student who "likes pistachio ice cream" or "has lived in another country."

22 Plan the first days of school down to the minute.

First teacher: "It was the longest day of my life."

Second teacher: "I couldn't believe it was already 3:00. The day just flew!"

What made the difference between these two first-day experiences? One word: planning.

The old teaching maxim is scary but true: What you do on the first day of school can make or break the entire school year. No matter how casual your personal style is, you cannot "wing" these first few days. You must plan, and then plan again.

To plan for the first day, start out with a painstakingly detailed schedule for the day. Calculate exactly how long you expect each activity to last. Cut that time in half and plan a second activity to fill the newly available time.

In addition to a detailed daily plan,

make sure that you have four or five "filler" activities planned for emergencies. First-week filler activities might include a word-find with students' names or a number puzzle using students' birthdays.

Remember, every moment of planning that you invest early in the school year will be returned to you in the successful year to come.

TIME	TASK	NOTES
8:30-8:40	Welcome students. Students begin opening activity.	· Interest Inventories: have inventories and pencils in Homework Folders on desks. · Personal license plates: have markers and paper available
8:40-8:45	Introduce myself	· Have name and class on board. · Write name in Greek. Tell about teaching English to grandmother.
8:45-8:55	Teach cue for getting attention	· Use "give me five" technique. · Practice by having kids ask each other questions from inventories. Use cue. Repeat.
8:55-9:30	Introduce discipline plan	· Have plan posted and copies in Homework Folders. · Make web of possible rules. · Discuss reasons for choosing five. · Discuss consequences. · Brainstorm lists of rewards.
9:30-9:40	Introduce Homework Folders	· Role play digging through backpack for homework. · List things they might put in folder. · Go through forms in folder that they need to return.
9:40-9:55	Introduce dismissal procedure	· Have procedure posted. · Practice, using clothing colors to dismiss. · Extra time: brainstorm other selection methods.
9:55	Dismiss for recess	· Use dismissal procedure. · Walk kids to playground.

Leave nothing to chance on the first days of school. Plan extra activities for each available time block.

23 Post the day's schedule and assignments.

You can cut down on distractions and interruptions simply by posting your daily schedule and assignments in a prominent place in the classroom. (See strategy 13.)

Keep your assignment list in the same place all year so that students always know where to look to find out what to do. If you are short on chalkboard space, you may want to purchase a large dry-erase board for the purpose. Use a different color of chalk or marker for each subject area or class (if it's math, it's in purple).

To help students plan their time, post a large wall calendar in a prominent position near the assignment list. On the calendar, record due dates for weekly assignments or major projects, as well as special activities such as field trips or performances.

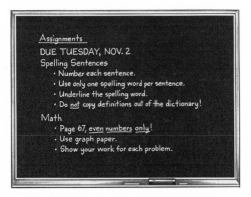

Assignments

DUE TUESDAY, NOV. 2

Spelling Sentences
· Number each sentence.
· Use only one spelling word per sentence.
· Underline the spelling word.
· Do _not_ copy definitions out of the dictionary!

Math
· Page 67, _even numbers only_!
· Use graph paper.
· Show your work for each problem.

Post your students' assignments in the same place each day.

24

Don't waste class time on housekeeping.

Don't let clerical tasks such as taking
attendance and distributing materials rob
you of precious instructional time. Protect
your students' learning time by finding
ways to complete these tasks with as little
disruption as possible.

Taking Attendance

✔ Do not waste the first few minutes of
the day taking attendance. Instead,
have an assignment ready for students
to complete as soon as they enter the
classroom (see strategy 17). Then
quietly take attendance as they work.

✔ Laminate your seating chart, or slip
it into a plastic protector. Use an
overhead (erasable) marker to mark
students who are absent.

✔ Write each student's name on a
clothespin and clip the pins around the

rim of a plastic bucket. As students come in the room, have them drop their clothespins into the container or clip them onto cards marked "Hot Lunch" and "Bag Lunch."

✔ Hang name tags by the door with two extra hooks labeled "Hot Lunch" and "Bag Lunch." As students come in, have them hang their tags on the appropriate hooks.

Distributing Materials

✔ Passing papers across rows to one side is less disruptive than passing them to the front.

✔ Designate one or two students each week to collect and pass out materials.

✔ Assign each student a number according to the order of names in your grade book. Have students write their numbers on their assignments and place them in numerical order as they hand them in.

✔ Keep a different colored folder for each subject you teach. Have students place their completed work in the appropriate folder.

✔ Use cartons or cubbies as mailboxes. Distribute all papers to the mailboxes before class begins.

✔ Have a "pickup" table by the door. Place materials on the table so that students can pick them up as they enter the classroom and drop them off as they leave.

25 Use "sponge" activities.

You are just about to start a lesson when you are called to the telephone. What do you do?

Sponge activities are short activities that you can use to keep students actively involved during odd moments like these. Many teachers also use sponges as opening assignments at the beginning of the day or as a quick skill reinforcement at the end of a lesson or the school day.

Write activity ideas on index cards and keep the card file within easy reach. Here are a few ideas to get you started:

✔ List as many states as you can.
✔ Draw your favorite animal.
✔ Make up three story problems using fractions.
✔ How many different ways can you use a paper clip? List them.

26   Plan to teach reading (no matter what subject you teach).

If you are a specialist or a secondary teacher, you probably don't think of yourself as a reading teacher. Think again. To succeed in any subject area, students must be able to read and understand the content. In fact, student achievement in all subject areas improves when students are given substantial amounts of time to read.

Plan to teach the vocabulary and comprehension skills your students need to master your subject matter. Set aside in-class time so that students can begin reading assignments and ask questions. Be alert to problems that individuals are having and make sure they receive the extra help they need. Finally, offer students the opportunity to read independently after completing assignments. They—and you—will soon find out that reading is its own reward!

27 Plan to teach problem solving.

No matter what grade or subject you teach, you can make your job easier by teaching your students how to solve problems. Students who know how to solve problems can take responsibility for their own learning. Because they can apply what they know from one context to another, they can "take the ball and run with it." As a result, you spend less time spoon-feeding information and more time inspiring achievement.

Look for ways that you can challenge your students to stretch their problem-solving abilities. For example:

✔ Use problem-solving strategies to solve classroom dilemmas. ("We've got too many people who want to use the computer at once. How can we solve this problem?")

✔ Challenge students to come up with alternative methods for solving problems. ("How else might the Patriots have gotten King George's attention?")

✔ Ask students to explain their thinking process. ("Show me how you figured out this answer.")

28

Provide time for student practice.

To achieve their goals, sports players and performers must practice. So it is with academic achievement: the more time your students spend working on the task at hand, the more likely they are to succeed. How can you increase the time your students have on each task? Here are a few suggestions:

- ✔ Post all assignments each day so that students can start to work immediately.
- ✔ Use 10- to 15-minute lessons for direct instruction.
- ✔ Divide instruction into sub-skills. Teach only one objective per lesson.
- ✔ Use as little class time as possible for clerical tasks such as taking attendance or distributing papers.
- ✔ Provide assignments that keep students actively engaged (not busywork). Students who are interested in their work are more likely to stay on task.

29

Learn the art of questioning.

How you ask a question can make a big difference in what—and whether—your students learn. Before you teach a lesson, list the questions you want to ask, and imagine your students' possible responses. Does your question require students to use higher-order thinking skills? Is it too simplistic or vague? Can you state it more clearly? Will students be able to see how the question is related to your objectives for the lesson?

Keep a list of good "question starters" handy. Questions that start with words like *compare, evaluate, imagine, predict,* and *what's your opinion* reinforce critical-thinking skills. Always ask the question *before* you call on a student. Then wait a full four seconds for the student to respond. This "wait time" is important. It gives students a chance to think through their answers and respond more carefully.

If a student has difficulty answering a question, try rephrasing or gently guiding the student toward the correct answer. Don't stay involved with one student too long, however. Keep the momentum of the lesson moving forward.

30 Establish guidelines for written work.

As students throughout the ages have known, teachers' pet peeves are different. What bugged last year's teacher might slide by this year. On the other hand, what slid by last year may make this year's teacher throw a fit.

Eliminate the guesswork for both you and your students. Tell them in no uncertain terms how you expect written work to be completed.

Give your students a model. Decide how you want students to head their papers (name, section number, date, and so on) and post the heading on the board. Specify where and how you want students' "thinking work" to be done. Post anonymous samples of model papers. Be specific about which writing tools are acceptable and which are not (not "in pen," but "in black or blue ink pen, no fluorescent gel pens").

31 **Use routines to avoid homework hassles.**

"You didn't give it to me." "I musta been in the bathroom when you handed that out." "My dog ate it."

Most students think that teachers give homework just to be mean. Little do they know that homework can be the bane of a teacher's existence as well as their own. A few simple routines can help you avoid homework hassles.

✔ Post all assignments on the board. Be specific. (Not "Spelling Sentences," but "Write 20 sentences, using one spelling word in each sentence.")

✔ Set aside time for students to write down assignments in their assignment notebooks.

✔ Make students accountable for handing in assignments. Designate a homework tray, basket, or shelf, and tell students,

"If it's not in the homework basket, it hasn't been completed."

✔ Establish a procedure for absent students making up work. Some teachers record assignments in an assignment log (card file or three-ring binder) and give students the responsibility for checking the log and making up any missed work.

✔ Divide long-term assignments into smaller, more manageable tasks, and give students due dates for each task.

✔ Give students in-class time to start on their homework so they have a chance to sort out any areas of confusion before they get home.

32

Give an immediate response whenever possible.

Ugh. Grading papers. You know you should correct papers as soon as possible. You know how valuable an immediate response can be. Still, more often than not, grading papers is a chore. You have 30, 90, 150 papers to grade. Immediate response? How? Here are some ideas to help you get closer to your ideal:

✔ Choose one assignment per subject per week that you will correct for diagnostic purposes. Have students self-correct all other assignments.

✔ Use your time for grading large assignments and projects. For small assignments, record only that students have completed the work.

✔ Assign students numbers according to the order of their names in your grade book. Have students write their numbers on the headings of their papers. Then check and record their assignments in order.

✔ Stagger your due dates. Schedule your assignments so that no two classes have assignments due on the same day.

33 Eliminate distractions and interruptions.

First there's Ramon's mom, bringing by his homework. Then there's Kira's assistant who wants to take her to the learning lab. After that, Ms. Chung sends a student to ask if you have any extra scissors handy.

Interruptions will be with you always, but you can cut down on the ones that bother you most. Here's how.

✔ Close the door. A closed door is not rude; it simply says, "We need some uninterrupted time."
✔ Teach your students to use nonverbal (hand) signals to avoid interrupting lessons. For example, holding up one finger could mean, "May I go to the bathroom?"
✔ Give students a signal for asking for help. Some teachers pass out self-sticking notes. A "sticky note" on the front of a desk means "I need help."

34 Move into cooperative group work gradually.

Most educators agree that cooperative grouping helps learning. In a well-structured cooperative group situation, students learn to take responsibility for their own and one another's learning; they learn to communicate with others to make decisions and settle conflicts; and they learn to value and work to improve their own and others' contributions to the group's goal.

Cooperative grouping is great, but there's a caveat: It works only if you and your students are ready for it. Check this readiness test before you make the move:

✔ Are classroom routines in place and functioning? (See strategy 4.)
✔ Is your discipline plan working? Do students understand the rules and consequences? (See strategy 9.)
✔ Look at your lesson objective. Does it make sense to have students work in cooperative groups toward that objective?

✔ Is there a way to build in a method of individual accountability for group members?

When you do choose to use cooperative grouping, plan your first grouping carefully.

✔ Make sure you have a clear lesson objective. Then list the tasks that must be completed to fulfill the objective. Assign that many students to each group.
✔ Assign groups. Do not have students self-select groups. Self-selecting can amount to a cruel popularity contest.
✔ Students will complain about their groupings. Assure them that the configuration of the groups will change.
✔ Use role-playing to teach cooperative skills, such as making group decisions, resolving conflicts, and taking responsibility for one's own work.

Post the procedures for working within a cooperative group:

1. Remember that you are responsible for the group's—not just your own—work.
2. Do your own job well.
3. Do not hesitate to ask for—and give— help from your group-mates. Remember, you are working as a team.
4. If you are stuck, designate one group-mate as a spokesperson who will sort out the problem with the teacher.
5. Recognize and use one another's strengths and abilities.

35 Test early and often.

Say the word "test," and people tend to think of end results: the final reckoning.

In most cases, however, "final" tests have limited usefulness. To be truly useful, a test should help you assess the needs of the students so that you can provide appropriate instruction. Think of yourself as a medical practitioner. Doctors test to see what's wrong, and then decide on a course of treatment. Testing can serve the same purpose for you.

Write your test before you teach your lesson. Think: *What do I want students to know or be able to do?* Decide on your lesson objectives (goals), and then write your test questions so that they correlate to the objectives. Use pretests and frequent interval testing to help you individualize instruction.

36 Know your students.

You know the kid. She's the one who sits back there in the middle of the middle row. She's a good kid. Doesn't say much. Turns in her work on time. Now . . . what was her name again?

The better you know your students, the more effective you will be as a teacher—it's as simple as that. Getting to know your students seems like an easy enough task—until you have 150 students to get to know.

Write each student's name, address, and family members' names on an index card and keep it in a Rolodex® file. If you have more than one class, use different colored cards for each class. Note students' achievements and difficulties on the cards. When it's time to talk frankly with parents at conference time, you'll be glad you did.

37

Try to speak with each student for a few moments each day.

The most powerful teaching tool you have at your disposal is your own attention. Just a few moments of your positive attention can go a long way toward building the relationships that are so critical to successful teaching.

- ✔ Make an effort to get to know the details of your students' lives. Ask students to write their name, a favorite book, their pets' names, or other interests on an index card. Use the information to relate students' learning to their "real" lives.
- ✔ Try to make one positive remark to each student each day.
- ✔ Never criticize a student's question. If necessary, redirect the question, but try to keep the lines of communication open.

38 Develop a "teacher look."

Chances are good that there is a teacher in your past who had "the look" down cold. Just the thought of that glare is probably enough to stop you in your tracks even now!

Don't let minor infractions disrupt the flow of your instruction. You can head off many problems simply by moving around the room and maintaining eye contact with students. Develop a "teacher look" and a quiet "teacher voice" that say you mean business. If you must confront a student, do so with as little fuss as possible:

✔ Speak softly, but firmly.
✔ Say the student's name.
✔ Describe the problem. In some cases, simply pointing to the appropriate rule on your discipline plan will be adequate warning.

✔ State the consequences. (See strategy 9.)
✔ Do not argue or negotiate. Simply remind the student that she chose to break the rule and restate the consequences.

39   Use humor.

There is an old saying that "he who laughs, lasts." This is certainly true in the classroom. Humor can break the ice and capture students' attention. A little laughter can relieve stress and, in a sticky situation, save your sanity.

You don't need to be a stand-up comedian to infuse some lighthearted humor into your classroom routines. Keep your eye out for school-related jokes, cartoons, and anecdotes, and stick them in a file for future reference. Post comic strips or funny quotations to discuss each week. Initiate a riddle of the day routine or ask students to help you create your own versions of David Letterman's "Top Ten" lists. Use silly props, accents, or "helpers" such as puppets for a change of pace. Do feel free to laugh at yourself, but never use humor at the expense of a student.

Add a little levity to your classroom by posting a daily cartoon or riddle.

40 **Use motivators.**

Think back on the last time you felt successful. What motivated you toward success? Was it money? Grades? An award? Most likely, your primary motivation was the achievement itself. For students, too, success is its own reward. (As one primary teacher puts it, "Stickers are great. Knowing how to read is even better.")

Even angry, discouraged, or "too cool to care" students like to succeed. Give them a chance to succeed by setting reasonable goals and objectives. Praise even the smallest successes. Then, when a student reaches a goal, celebrate. Celebrations might include:

✔ a special activity (free reading time, math games, etc.)
✔ preferred seating
✔ a phone call to the student's parent
✔ "student of the week" status

41

Establish clearly when and how you can be contacted.

It's been a long, rough day. You are just drifting off to sleep when the telephone rings. It is Grace's mom, with just a couple of "issues" she would like to discuss.

Study after study confirms what most teachers already know: students learn best when their parents and teachers work together as a team. You know you must be accessible to parents. It's part of your job. But you need not discuss "issues" with a parent at 11 o'clock at night. For new teachers, it's often difficult to know where to draw the line. The following guidelines may help:

✔ Decide when and how you want to be contacted *before* the school year begins or a parent asks. Some teachers (and parents) feel most comfortable communicating by e-mail. Others will take phone calls at school, but not at home.

Still others don't mind chatting at home, but only during certain hours.

✔ Take the initiative to call parents with good news. The more positive interaction you have, the easier it will be to work out problems.

✔ If there is a problem, contact the parent immediately. Describe the behavior specifically. (Not "Susie is having problems controlling her temper," but "Susie lost her temper and threw a chair at another child this morning.")

✔ Keep the conversation short—no longer than fifteen minutes. If necessary, suggest that you arrange another phone call or meeting to continue the discussion.

42

Use a regular newsletter to communicate with parents.

Most parents would love to support the work you are doing with their children. They simply don't know how. At the same time, your professional knowledge could help parents who are struggling with the day-to-day challenges of raising children in a sometimes frightening world. A weekly newsletter can help you give—and get—the support both you and your students' parents need.

What makes one newsletter a "cut above" another is the quality of information it contains. Leave out the smiley faces and hearts. Give parents real information that relates to your students and their success at school. Write your newsletter as if you were writing to a fellow professional. You are. After all, you are both in the business of caring for the same child.

✔ Use your lesson objectives to give parents specific information about the curriculum. Instead of "We'll be studying rainforests," try "I will expect students to be able to name the levels of the rainforest environment and give examples of wildlife found in each level."

✔ Talk about recent child development research that affects the students at your grade level. A little information about child development can be very comforting to the parent who thinks that his sixth grader is the only one who has ever "acted like this."

✔ Give two or three activities or tips on how parents can help students succeed in school. Be specific. Not "Practice addition," but "Play cards, and let your child keep score." Not "Read with your child," but "Here's what to do when your child comes to a word she doesn't know."

✔ Ask an ESL or foreign language teacher to help you translate your letter for parents who don't speak English.

✔ Finally, proofread your letter—better still, have someone else proofread it. Make sure that the print is clear, and that spelling and grammar are correct.

43   **Overplan conferences.**

Parent conferences are nerve-wracking for both parents and teachers. Both parties are sure they will be blamed for *something!*

Plan for a parent conference the way you would for a job interview or the first day of school. The more comfortable you are with your facts, the easier the conference will go. Here are a few guidelines:

✔ Review the names of the student's family members (see strategy 36). Use formal titles when addressing parents unless you are told *by them* to do otherwise.

✔ Be prepared with a portfolio of the student's work and your own notes on the student's behavior and achievement. (See strategies 8 and 10.)

✔ Begin and end each conference with positive statements about the student.

✔ Prepare a handout for frequently asked questions (e.g., reading lists or your homework policy).

✔ Take notes and send a written confirmation of any decisions made during the conference.

✔ Keep your conferences on schedule. If necessary, set up a second conference with parents who need additional time.

44 Make friends with the custodial and secretarial staff.

Make no mistake about it: secretaries and custodians run the school. Most likely, they have seen administrators and teachers come and go. Having been there awhile, they know the students better, have a more thorough handle on the schedule, and are simply more in tune with the rhythms of the school than others in the building.

Ask for help—only school-related help—respectfully. Use formal titles and the person's job description to guide your requests unless you are told *by the person* to do otherwise. These professionals are your first, best resources. They will help you out of countless binds this year and for many years to come.

45 Get to know your principal (and give your principal a chance to get to know you).

Too often, new teachers isolate themselves from their colleagues at just the time when they most need camaraderie and support. To be a successful teacher, you must have your principal's support. The first step in gaining that support is establishing positive communication.

✔ Figure out who's the boss. In small schools, your boss—the person who has the power to support you and also to evaluate you—will likely be the principal. In larger schools, it may be the assistant principal or a department head.

✔ Invite the principal to your classroom. The more a principal knows about you, the more comfortable he or she is supporting you. Most new teachers would rather die than have the principal visit their classroom. Take some of the edge off the fear by structuring the moment yourself. Most principals are former teachers who miss the time they once had with students. Invite your principal to read with your students, to play math games, or to help with Internet research. You, your students, and your principal will be glad you did.

✔ Whenever you send a newsletter to parents, slip a copy into your principal's mailbox.

✔ Don't be afraid to blow your own horn. Keep a portfolio of your best work—lesson plans, student presentations, interactive bulletin boards (take photos). Take the portfolio to every meeting you have with the principal.

✔ Choose your battles. Think, *Is there some other way or someone else who can help me solve this problem?*

✔ Find out how and when you will be evaluated. New teachers often feel that asking for help is a sign that they're not doing well in their jobs. You have a right to know the criteria on which you will be evaluated so that you can ask for help when you need it.

46 Treat fellow teachers with respect.

There is no such thing as a self-contained classroom these days. Even in the elementary grades, teaching assistants come and go, and specialists compete for class time. Try to keep in mind that each of these teachers, like you, has a job to do. Try also to remember that you are all in this together. Above all, keep some fundamental manners in mind:

✔ Do not pull your students from another teacher's class unless absolutely necessary.

✔ Acknowledge other teachers' successes. Be generous.

✔ Do not gossip. This seems like an easy rule to follow, but it's not.

✔ Never criticize another teacher in front of students. Never.

47 Seek help from others.

Teachers value their autonomy. As a new teacher, you may feel that you should be able to "go it alone." But going it alone can be a very lonely experience. Don't fall into that trap. If you want to survive the first year of teaching, let other people help you.

✔ Seek advice when you need it. Remember that support staff such as library media specialists, technology specialists, and exceptional needs teachers are there to help *you* as well as the students.

✔ Keep in touch with other first-year teachers, either from your university or within your school system. Arrange to go out to dinner or take a hike together. You will be surprised at how many concerns you have in common.

✔ Cultivate professional affiliations. If your school won't pay for your membership to professional organizations in your field, do so yourself. These organizations can give you both instructional and career guidance when you need it most.

✔ Take advantage of as many professional development opportunities as you can. Go to workshops and take in-service classes. You may be exhausted, but hearing the stories of others and learning new strategies will help revitalize you.

48

Know when to say "no."

School administrators count on teachers to provide "coverage" or instruction for many extracurricular activities. If you are truly interested in the subject—be it rocketry, soccer, or weaving—you may find that you enjoy getting to know your students, and others, in a different context. But if you are simply "covering" an activity, you may find the experience to be a drain on both your time and energy.

Keep in mind that the first year of teaching is a very stressful year, and that your own class is your first responsibility. You may feel pressured to say "yes" when you really want to say "no." These guidelines will help you make the decision:

✔ Know your contractual obligations.
✔ Practice saying, "I'd love to, but I have my hands full right now with my classroom responsibilities."

✔ Be prepared with your answer *before* you are asked. If you are caught off guard, say, "Let me think about it and get back to you."

✔ Don't feel guilty about saying "no." Remember that 50 percent of teachers leave the profession within seven years. Protect yourself and your time so that you are part of the 50 percent who survive—and thrive.

49 Pat yourself on the back at least once a day.

Keep your eyes on the prize. No matter how thankless your job seems at times, your students do need you. Think hard about the objectives of your lessons so that you know the value of what you are teaching. Then find one thing—just one—that you've done right each day and congratulate yourself for it.

Above all, hang in there. The first year of teaching is always hard—sometimes miserable. But the second year is almost always better. And for many teachers, each new year brings new successes and greater joy in teaching.

First-Week Assignments
That Make Great Bulletin Boards

✔ Self-portraits: save these to compare with portraits done at the end of the year.

✔ Hand-drawn book covers for favorite books.

✔ Guess who: post current photos and baby photos, and have students try to match them.

✔ Interest inventories for each student: have students try to guess whose inventory is whose.

✔ Name poems: students write self-describing words or phrases that begin with each letter of their names.

✔ Personal timelines or coats of arms.

✔ Graphs from a class opinion poll or survey.

✔ Random acts of kindness: have each student write his or her name and a recent act of kindness on an index card.

Must-Have Classroom Supplies

✓ attendance and/or grade book
brads
✓ calendar
✓ chalk (white and colored)
✓ chalkboard eraser
✓ clock
computer disks
construction paper
✓ crayons
drawing paper
erasers
file folders
first-aid kit with latex gloves
glue or glue sticks
hole punch
markers (thick and thin)
masking tape
paper clips
✓ paper towels
✓ pencils and pens
poster board and chart paper

Must-Have Classroom Supplies
(continued)

rubber bands
rulers
scissors
sponge and cleanser
stapler and staples
tape (regular and two-sided)
thumbtacks
timer
tissues
writing paper
yardstick

Helpful Books for New Teachers

✔ *The First Days of School* by Harry K. Wong and Rosemary T. Wong (Harry K. Wong Publications, Inc., 1998)

✔ *First-Class Teacher* by Canter and Associates (Canter and Associates, Inc., 1998)

✔ *Your First Year of Teaching and Beyond* by Ellen L. Kronowitz (Addison Wesley Longman Inc., 1998)

✔ *Classroom Teacher's Survival Guide* by Ronald L. Partin (The Center for Applied Research in Education, 1995)

Helpful Web Sites for New Teachers

Beginning Teacher Tips
http://www.inspiringteachers.com/tips/
index/index.html

The Educational Resources Information
Center (ERIC)
http://www.accesseric.org/

Firstyears: A Web Site for Beginning and
Student Teachers
http://www.ametro.net/~teachers/home.
html

National Education Association's Works 4
Me Tips Library
http://www.nea.org/helpfrom/growing/
works4me/library.html

Order Today!

Item No.	Quantity	Price Each	Amount
1.			
2.			
3.			

Order Total	Shipping
Up to $30.00	$4.95
$31.00 to $100.00	$7.95
$101.00 and above	$10.95

*Books are taxable in the following states:
CA 7.25%
LA 4.00%
NC 6.00%
SC 5.00%

+ Shipping _____

Subtotal _____

Sales Tax* _____

TOTAL _____

Ship To: (Please use street address only)

Name _____

Title _____Grade(s) _____

School/District _____

Street Address _____

City _____ State _____ ZIP _____

Phone (___) _____

Method of Payment:

❑ Check enclosed (payable to School Renaissance Institute)

❑ Bill my school (purchase order required**) P.O. # _____

❑ Bill my district (purchase order required**) P.O. # _____

❑ MasterCard® ❑ VISA® ❑ American Express®

The following information is required for credit card orders:

Account No. _____

Exp. Date _____

Signature _____

Home Phone (___) _____

** You may mail or fax us a fully executed purchase order with approved number. Purchase orders are billed net 30 days. Sorry, we cannot accept oral purchase orders.

Pricing Information: All prices are F.O.B. Madison, WI. Prices are effective March 1, 2000, and are subject to change without notice.

Warranty/Replacement: Books are guaranteed to be free from defects in materials and workmanship. School Renaissance Institute will replace books found to be defective.

4184.0700